The Cup: A Tragedy by Lord Alfred Tennyson

Alfred Tennyson was born on August 6th, 1809, in Somersby, Lincolnshire, the fourth of twelve children.

Most of Tennyson's early education was under the direction of his father, although he did spend four unhappy years at a nearby grammar school. He left home in 1827 to join his elder brothers at Trinity College, Cambridge, more to escape his father than a desire for serious academic work. At Trinity he was living for the first time among young men of his own age who knew little of his problems. He was delighted to make new friends; he was handsome, intelligent, humorous, a gifted impersonator and soon at the center of those interested in poetry and conversation.

That same year, he and his brother Charles published Poems by Two Brothers. Although the poems in the book were of teenage quality, they attracted the attention of the "Apostles," a select undergraduate literary club led by Arthur Hallam. The "Apostles" provided Tennyson with friendship and confidence. Hallam and Tennyson became the best of friends; they toured Europe together in 1830 and again in 1832. Hallam's sudden death in 1833 greatly affected the young poet. The long elegy In Memoriam and many of Tennyson's other poems are tributes to Hallam.

In 1830, Tennyson published Poems, Chiefly Lyrical and in 1832 he published a second volume entitled simply Poems. Some reviewers condemned these books as "affected" and "obscure." Tennyson, stung by the reviews, would not publish another book for nine years.

In 1836, he became engaged to Emily Sellwood. When he lost his inheritance on a failed investment in 1840, the engagement was cancelled.

In 1842, however, Tennyson's Poems [in two volumes] was a tremendous critical and popular success. In 1850, with the publication of In Memoriam, Tennyson's reputation was pre-eminent. He was also selected as Poet Laureate in succession to Wordsworth and, to complete a wonderful year, he married Emily Sellwood.

At the age of 41, Tennyson had established himself as the most popular poet of the Victorian era. The money from his poetry [at times exceeding 10,000 pounds per year] allowed him to purchase a home in the country and to write in relative seclusion. His appearance—a large and bearded man, he regularly wore a cloak and a broad brimmed hat—enhanced his notoriety.

In 1859, Tennyson published the first poems of Idylls of the Kings, which sold more than 10,000 copies in a fortnight. In 1884, he accepted a peerage, becoming Alfred Lord Tennyson.

On October 6th, 1892, an hour or so after midnight, surrounded by his family, he died at Aldworth. It is said that the moonlight was streaming through the window and Tennyson himself was holding open a volume of Shakespeare.

He was buried in Westminster Abbey.

Index of Contents

DRAMATIS PERSONAE
GALATIANS:
SYNORIX, an ex-Tetrarch.
SINNATUS, a Tetrarch.
Attendant.
Boy.
Maid.
PHOEBE.
CAMMA, wife of Sinnatus, afterwards Priestess in the Temple of Artemis.

ROMANS:
ANTONIUS, a Roman General.
PUBLIUS.
Nobleman.
Messenger.

ACT I

SCENE I

Distant View of a City of Galatia.

As the curtain rises, **PRIESTESSES** are heard singing in the Temple. **BOY** discovered on a pathway among Rocks, picking grapes. A party of **ROMAN SOLDIERS**, guarding a prisoner in chains, come down the pathway and exeunt.

Enter **SYNORIX** [looking round]. Singing ceases.

SYNORIX
Pine, beech and plane, oak, walnut, apricot,
Vine, cypress, poplar, myrtle, bowering in
The city where she dwells. She past me here
Three years ago when I was flying from
My Tetrarchy to Rome. I almost touch'd her—

A maiden slowly moving on to music
Among her maidens to this Temple—O Gods!
She is my fate—else wherefore has my fate
Brought me again to her own city?—married
Since—married Sinnatus, the Tetrarch here—
But if he be conspirator, Rome will chain,
Or slay him. I may trust to gain her then
When I shall have my tetrarchy restored
By Rome, our mistress, grateful that I show'd her
The weakness and the dissonance of our clans,
And how to crush them easily. Wretched race!
And once I wish'd to scourge them to the bones.
But in this narrow breathing-time of life
Is vengeance for its own sake worth the while,
If once our ends are gain'd? and now this cup—
I never felt such passion for a woman.

[Brings out a cup and scroll from under his cloak.

What have I written to her?

[Reading the scroll.

'To the admired Gamma, wife of Sinnatus, the Tetrarch, one who years ago, himself an adorer of our great goddess, Artemis, beheld you afar off worshipping in her Temple, and loved you for it, sends you this cup rescued from the burning of one of her shrines in a city thro' which he past with the Roman army: it is the cup we use in our marriages. Receive it from one who cannot at present write himself other than   'A GALATIAN SERVING BY FORCE IN THE ROMAN LEGION.'

[Turns and looks up to **BOY**.

Boy, dost thou know the house of Sinnatus?

BOY
These grapes are for the house of Sinnatus—
Close to the Temple.

SYNORIX
Yonder?

BOY
Yes.

SYNORIX [aside]
That I
With all my range of women should yet shun
To meet her face to face at once! My boy,

[BOY comes down rocks to him.

Take thou this letter and this cup to Camma,
The wife of Sinnatus.

BOY
Going or gone to-day
To hunt with Sinnatus.

SYNORIX
That matters not.
Take thou this cup and leave it at her doors.

[Gives the cup and scroll to the Boy.

BOY
I will, my lord.

[Takes his basket of grapes and exit.

Enter **ANTONIUS**

ANTONIUS [meeting the **BOY** as he goes out]
Why, whither runs the boy?
Is that the cup you rescued from the fire?

SYNORIX
I send it to the wife of Sinnatus,
One half besotted in religious rites.
You come here with your soldiers to enforce
The long-withholden tribute: you suspect
This Sinnatus of playing patriotism,
Which in your sense is treason. You have yet
No proof against him: now this pious cup
Is passport to their house, and open arms
To him who gave it; and once there I warrant
I worm thro' all their windings.

ANTONIUS
If you prosper,
Our Senate, wearied of their tetrarchies,
Their quarrels with themselves, their spites at Rome,
Is like enough to cancel them, and throne
One king above them all, who shall be true
To the Roman: and from what I heard in Rome,
This tributary crown may fall to you.

SYNORIX

The king, the crown! their talk in Rome? is it so?

[**ANTONIUS** nods.

Well—I shall serve Galatia taking it,
And save her from herself, and be to Rome
More faithful than a Roman.

[Turns and sees **CAMMA** coming.

Stand aside,
Stand aside; here she comes!

[Watching **CAMMA** as she enters with her **MAID**.

GAMMA [to **MAID**]
Where is he, girl?

MAID
You know the waterfall
That in the summer keeps the mountain side,
But after rain o'erleaps a jutting rock
And shoots three hundred feet.

CAMMA
The stag is there?

MAID
Seen in the thicket at the bottom there
But yester-even.

GAMMA
Good then, we will climb
The mountain opposite and watch the chase.

[They descend the rocks and exeunt.

SYNORIX [watching her]
[Aside.] The bust of Juno and the brows and eyes
Of Venus; face and form unmatchable!

ANTONIUS
Why do you look at her so lingeringly?

SYNORIX
To see if years have changed her.

ANTONIUS [sarcastically]

Love her, do you?

SYNORIX
I envied Sinnatus when he married her.

ANTONIUS
She knows it? Ha!

SYNORIX
She—no, nor ev'n my face.

ANTONIUS
Nor Sinnatus either?

SYNORIX
No, nor Sinnatus.

ANTONIUS
Hot-blooded! I have heard them say in Rome.
That your own people cast you from their bounds,
For some unprincely violence to a woman,
As Rome did Tarquin.

SYNORIX
Well, if this were so,
I here return like Tarquin—for a crown.

ANTONIUS
And may be foil'd like Tarquin, if you follow
Not the dry light of Rome's straight-going policy,
But the fool-fire of love or lust, which well
May make you lose yourself, may even drown you
In the good regard of Rome.

SYNORIX
Tut—fear me not;
I ever had my victories among women.
I am most true to Rome.

ANTONIUS [aside]
I hate the man!
What filthy tools our Senate works with! Still
I must obey them. [Aloud.] Fare you well.

[Going.

SYNORIX
Farewell!

ANTONIUS [stopping]
A moment! If you track this Sinnatus
In any treason, I give you here an order

[Produces a paper.

To seize upon him. Let me sign it. [Signs it.] There
'Antonius leader of the Roman Legion.'

[Hands the paper to **SYNORIX** Goes up pathway and exit.

SYNORIX
Woman again!—but I am wiser now.
No rushing on the game—the net,—the net.

[Shouts of 'Sinnatus! Sinnatus!' Then horn. Looking off stage.]

He comes, a rough, bluff, simple-looking fellow.
If we may judge the kernel by the husk,
Not one to keep a woman's fealty when
Assailed by Craft and Love. I'll join with him:
I may reap something from him—come upon her
Again, perhaps, to-day—her. Who are with him?
I see no face that knows me. Shall I risk it?
I am a Roman now, they dare not touch me.
I will.

Enter **SINNATUS, HUNTSMEN** and hounds.

Fair Sir, a happy day to you!
You reck but little of the Roman here,
While you can take your pastime in the woods.

SINNATUS
Ay, ay, why not? What would you with me, man?

SYNORIX
I am a life-long lover of the chase,
And tho' a stranger fain would be allow'd
To join the hunt.

SINNATUS
Your name?

SYNORIX
Strato, my name.

SINNATU
No Roman name?

SYNORIX
A Greek, my lord; you know
That we Galatians are both Greek and Gaul.
[Shouts and horns in the distance

SINNATUS
Hillo, the stag! [To **SYNORIX**] What, you are all unfurnish'd?
Give him a bow and arrows—follow—follow.
[Exit, followed by Huntsmen.

SYNORIX
Slowly but surely—till I see my way.
It is the one step in the dark beyond
Our expectation, that amazes us.
[Distant shouts and horns.
Hillo! Hillo!

[Exit **SYNORIX** Shouts and horns.

SCENE II.

—A Room in the Tetrarch's House.

Frescoed figures on the walls. Evening. Moonlight outside. A couch with cushions on it. A small table with flagon of wine, cups, plate of grapes, etc., also the cup of Scene I. A chair with drapery on it.

CAMMA enters, and opens' curtains of window.

CAMMA
No Sinnatus yet—and there the rising moon.

[Takes up a cithern and sits on couch. Plays and sings.

'Moon on the field and the foam,
Moon on the waste and the wold,
Moon bring him home, bring him home
Safe from the dark and the cold,
Home, sweet moon, bring him home,
Home with the flock to the fold—
Safe from the wolf'——

[Listening.] Is he coming? I thought I heard

A footstep. No not yet. They say that Rome
Sprang from a wolf. I fear my dear lord mixt
With some conspiracy against the wolf.
This mountain shepherd never dream'd of Rome.
[Sings.] 'Safe from the wolf to the fold'——
And that great break of precipice that runs
Thro' all the wood, where twenty years ago
Huntsman, and hound, and deer were all neck-broken!
Nay, here he comes.

Enter **SINNATUS** followed by **SYNORIX**

SINNATUS [angrily]
I tell thee, my good fellow,
My arrow struck the stag.

SYNORIX
But was it so?
Nay, you were further off: besides the wind
Went with my arrow.

SINNATUS
I am sure I struck him.

SYNORIX
And I am just as sure, my lord, I struck him.
[Aside.] And I may strike your game when you are gone.

CAMMA
Come, come, we will not quarrel about the stag.
I have had a weary day in watching you.
Yours must have been a wearier. Sit and eat,
And take a hunter's vengeance on the meats.

SINNATUS
No, no—we have eaten—we are heated. Wine!

CAMMA
Who is our guest?

SINNATUS.
Strato he calls himself.

[**CAMMA** offers wine to **SYNORIX**, while **SINNATUS** helps himself.

SINNATUS
I pledge you, Strato.   [Drinks.

SYNORIX
And I you, my lord.   [Drinks.

SINNATUS [seeing the cup sent to **CAMMA**]
What's here?

CAMMA
A strange gift sent to me to-day.
A sacred cup saved from a blazing shrine
Of our great Goddess, in some city where
Antonius past. I had believed that Rome
Made war upon the peoples not the Gods.

SYNORIX
Most like the city rose against Antonius,
Whereon he fired it, and the sacred shrine
By chance was burnt along with it.

SINNATUS
Had you then
No message with the cup?

CAMMA
Why, yes, see here.
[Gives him the scroll.

SINNATUS [reads]
'To the admired Camma,—beheld you afar off—loved you—sends you this cup—the cup we use in our marriages—cannot at present write himself other than 'A GALATIAN SERVING BY FORCE IN THE ROMAN LEGION.'

Serving by force! Were there no boughs to hang on,
Rivers to drown in? Serve by force? No force
Could make me serve by force.

SYNORIX
How then, my lord?
The Roman is encampt without your city—
The force of Rome a thousand-fold our own.
Must all Galatia hang or drown herself?
And you a Prince and Tetrarch in this province—

SINNATUS
Province!

SYNORIX
Well, well, they call it so in Rome.

SINNATUS [angrily]
Province!

SYNORIX
A noble anger! but Antonius
To-morrow will demand your tribute—you,
Can you make war? Have you alliances?
Bithynia, Pontus, Paphlagonia?
We have had our leagues of old with Eastern kings.
There is my hand—if such a league there be.
What will you do?

SINNATUS
Not set myself abroach
And run my mind out to a random guest
Who join'd me in the hunt. You saw my hounds
True to the scent; and we have two-legg'd dogs
Among us who can smell a true occasion,
And when to bark and how.

SYNORIX
My good Lord Sinnatus,
I once was at the hunting of a lion.
Roused by the clamour of the chase he woke,
Came to the front of the wood—his monarch mane
Bristled about his quick ears—he stood there
Staring upon the hunter. A score of dogs
Gnaw'd at his ankles: at the last he felt
The trouble of his feet, put forth one paw,
Slew four, and knew it not, and so remain'd
Staring upon the hunter: and this Rome
Will crush you if you wrestle with her; then
Save for some slight report in her own Senate
Scarce know what she has done.
[Aside.] Would I could move him,
Provoke him any way! [Aloud.] The Lady Camma,
Wise I am sure as she is beautiful,
Will close with me that to submit at once
Is better than a wholly-hopeless war,
Our gallant citizens murder'd all in vain,
Son, husband, brother gash'd to death in vain,
And the small state more cruelly trampled on
Than had she never moved.

CAMMA
Sir, I had once
A boy who died a babe; but were he living
And grown to man and Sinnatus will'd it, I

Would set him in the front rank of the fight
With scarce a pang. [Rises.] Sir, if a state submit
At once, she may be blotted out at once
And swallow'd in the conqueror's chronicle.
Whereas in wars of freedom and defence
The glory and grief of battle won or lost
Solders a race together—yea—tho' they fail,
The names of those who fought and fell are like
A bank'd-up fire that flashes out again
From century to century, and at last
May lead them on to victory—I hope so—
Like phantoms of the Gods.

SINNATUS
Well spoken, wife.

SYNORIX [bowing]
Madam, so well I yield.

SINNATUS
I should not wonder
If Synorix, who has dwelt three years in Rome
And wrought his worst against his native land.
Returns with this Antonius.

SYNORIX
What is Synorix?

SINNATUS
Galatian, and not know? This Synorix
Was Tetrarch here, and tyrant also—did
Dishonour to our wives.

SYNORIX
Perhaps you judge him
With feeble charity: being as you tell me
Tetrarch, there might be willing wives enough
To feel dishonour, honour.

CAMMA
Do not say so.
I know of no such wives in all Galatia.
There may be courtesans for aught I know
Whose life is one dishonour.

Enter **ATTENDANT**.

ATTENDANT [aside]

My lord, the men!

SINNATUS [aside]
Our anti-Roman faction?

ATTENDANT [aside]
Ay, my lord.

SYNORIX [overhearing]
[Aside.] I have enough—their anti-Roman faction.

SINNATUS [aloud]
Some friends of mine would speak with me without.
You, Strato, make good cheer till I return.

[Exit.

SYNORIX
I have much to say, no time to say it in.
First, lady, know myself am that Galatian
Who sent the cup.

CAMMA
I thank you from my heart.

SYNORIX
Then that I serve with Rome to serve Galatia.
That is my secret: keep it, or you sell me
To torment and to death.   [Coming closer.
For your ear only—
I love you—for your love to the great Goddess.
The Romans sent me here a spy upon you,
To draw you and your husband to your doom.
I'd sooner die than do it.
[Takes out paper given him by Antonius.
This paper sign'd
Antonius—will you take it, read it? there!

CAMMA
[Reads.] 'You are to seize on Sinnatus,—if—'

SYNORIX [Snatches paper.]
No more.
What follows is for no wife's eyes. O Camma,
Rome has a glimpse of this conspiracy;
Rome never yet hath spar'd conspirator.
Horrible! flaying, scourging, crucifying—

CAMMA
I am tender enough. Why do you practise on me?

SYNORIX
Why should I practise on you? How you wrong me!
I am sure of being every way malign'd.
And if you should betray me to your husband—

CAMMA
Will you betray him by this order?

SYNORIX
See,
I tear it all to pieces, never dream'd
Of acting on it.   [Tears the paper.

CAMMA
I owe you thanks for ever.

SYNORIX
Hath Sinnatus never told you of this plot?

CAMMA
What plot?

SYNORIX
A child's sand-castle on the beach
For the next wave—all seen,—all calculated,
All known by Rome. No chance for Sinnatus.

CAMMA
Why said you not as much to my brave Sinnatus?

SYNORIX
Brave—ay—too brave, too over-confident,
Too like to ruin himself, and you, and me!
Who else, with this black thunderbolt of Rome
Above him, would have chased the stag to-day
In the full face of all the Roman camp?
A miracle that they let him home again,
Not caught, maim'd, blinded him.

[**CAMMA** shudders.

[Aside.] I have made her tremble.
[Aloud.] I know they mean to torture him to death.
I dare not tell him how I came to know it;
I durst not trust him with—my serving Rome

To serve Galatia: you heard him on the letter.
Not say as much? I all but said as much.
I am sure I told him that his plot was folly.
I say it to you—you are wiser—Rome knows all,
But you know not the savagery of Rome.

CAMMA

O—have you power with Rome? use it for him!

SYNORIX

Alas! I have no such power with Rome. All that
Lies with Antonius.

[As if struck by a sudden thought. Comes over to her.

He will pass to-morrow
In the gray dawn before the Temple doors.
You have beauty,—O great beauty,—and Antonius,
So gracious toward women, never yet
Flung back a woman's prayer. Plead to him,
I am sure you will prevail.

CAMMA

Still—I should tell
My husband.

SYNORIX

Will he let you plead for him
To a Roman?

CAMMA

I fear not.

SYNORIX

Then do not tell him.
Or tell him, if you will, when you return,
When you have charm'd our general into mercy,
And all is safe again. O dearest lady,

[Murmurs of 'Synorix! Synorix!' heard outside.

Think,—torture,—death,—and come.

CAMMA

I will, I will.
And I will not betray you.

SYNORIX [aside]

[As **SINNATUS** enters.] Stand apart.

Enter **SINNATUS** and **ATTENDANT.**

SINNATUS
Thou art that Synorix! One whom thou hast wrong'd
Without there, knew thee with Antonius.
They howl for thee, to rend thee head from limb.

SYNORIX
I am much malign'd. I thought to serve Galatia.

SINNATUS
Serve thyself first, villain! They shall not harm
My guest within my house. There! [points to door] there! this door
Opens upon the forest! Out, begone!
Henceforth I am thy mortal enemy.

SYNORIX
However I thank thee [draws his sword]; thou hast
saved my life.

[Exit.

SINNATUS [To **ATTENDANT**]
Return and tell them Synorix is not here.

[Exit **ATTENDANT**.

What did that villain Synorix say to you?

GAMMA
Is he—that—Synorix?

SINNATUS
Wherefore should you doubt it?
One of the men there knew him.

CAMMA
Only one,
And he perhaps mistaken in the face.

SINNATUS
Come, come, could he deny it? What did he say?

CAMMA
What should he say?

SINNATUS
What should he say, my wife!
He should say this, that being Tetrarch once
His own true people cast him from their doors
Like a base coin.

CAMMA
Not kindly to them?

SINNATUS
Kindly?
O the most kindly Prince in all the world!
Would clap his honest citizens on the back,
Bandy their own rude jests with them, be curious
About the welfare of their babes, their wives,
O ay—their wives—their wives. What should he say?
He should say nothing to my wife if I
Were by to throttle him! He steep'd himself
In all the lust of Rome. How should you guess
What manner of beast it is?

CAMMA
Yet he seem'd kindly,
And said he loathed the cruelties that Rome
Wrought on her vassals.

SINNATUS
Did he, honest man?

CAMMA
And you, that seldom brook the stranger here,
Have let him hunt the stag with you to-day.

SINNATUS
I warrant you now, he said he struck the stag.

CAMMA
Why no, he never touch'd upon the stag.

SINNATUS
Why so I said, my arrow. Well, to sleep.
[Goes to close door.

CAMMA
Nay, close not yet the door upon a night
That looks half day.

SINNATUS

True; and my friends may spy him
And slay him as he runs.

CAMMA
He is gone already.
Oh look,—yon grove upon the mountain,—white
In the sweet moon as with a lovelier snow!
But what a blotch of blackness underneath!
Sinnatus, you remember—yea, you must,
That there three years ago—the vast vine-bowers
Ran to the summit of the trees, and dropt
Their streamers earthward, which a breeze of May
Took ever and anon, and open'd out
The purple zone of hill and heaven; there
You told your love; and like the swaying vines—
Yea,—with our eyes,—our hearts, our prophet hopes
Let in the happy distance, and that all
But cloudless heaven which we have found together
In our three married years! You kiss'd me there
For the first time. Sinnatus, kiss me now.

SINNATUS
First kiss. [Kisses her.] There then. You talk almost as if it
Might be the last.

CAMMA
Will you not eat a little?

SINNATUS
No, no, we found a goat-herd's hut and shared
His fruits and milk. Liar! You will believe
Now that he never struck the stag—a brave one
Which you shall see to-morrow.

CAMMA
I rise to-morrow
In the gray dawn, and take this holy cup
To lodge it in the shrine of Artemis.

SINNATUS
Good!

CAMMA
If I be not back in half an hour,
Come after me.

SINNATUS
What! is there danger?

CAMMA
Nay,
None that I know: 'tis but a step from here
To the Temple.

SINNATUS
All my brain is full of sleep.
Wake me before you go, I'll after you—
After me now!   [Closes door and exit.

CAMMA [drawing curtains]
Your shadow. Synorix—
His face was not malignant, and he said
That men malign'd him. Shall I go? Shall I go?
Death, torture—
'He never yet flung back a woman's prayer'—
I go, but I will have my dagger with me.

[Exit.

SCENE III

—Same as Scene I. Dawn.

Music and Singing in the Temple.

Enter **SYNORIX** watchfully, after him **PUBLIUS** and **SOLDIERS.**

SYNORIX
Publius!

PUBLIUS
Here!

SYNORIX
Do you remember what
I told you?

PUBLIUS
When you cry 'Rome, Rome,' to seize
On whomsoever may be talking with you,
Or man, or woman, as traitors unto Rome.

SYNORIX
Right. Back again. How many of you are there?

PUBLIUS
Some half a score.

[Exeunt **SOLDIERS** and **PUBLIUS**.

SYNORIX
I have my guard about me.
I need not fear the crowd that hunted me
Across the woods, last night. I hardly gain'd
The camp at midnight. Will she come to me
Now that she knows me Synorix? Not if Sinnatus
Has told her all the truth about me. Well,
I cannot help the mould that I was cast in.
I fling all that upon my fate, my star.
I know that I am genial, I would be
Happy, and make all others happy so
They did not thwart me. Nay, she will not come.
Yet if she be a true and loving wife
She may, perchance, to save this husband. Ay!
See, see, my white bird stepping toward the snare.
Why now I count it all but miracle,
That this brave heart of mine should shake me so,
As helplessly as some unbearded boy's
When first he meets his maiden in a bower.

Enter **CAMMA** [with cup]

SYNORIX
The lark first takes the sunlight on his wing,
But you, twin sister of the morning star,
Forelead the sun.

CAMMA
Where is Antonius?

SYNORIX
Not here as yet. You are too early for him.

[She crosses towards Temple.

SYNORIX
Nay, whither go you now?

CAMMA
To lodge this cup
Within the holy shrine of Artemis,
And so return.

SYNORIX
To find Antonius here.

[She goes into the Temple, he looks after her.

The loveliest life that ever drew the light
From heaven to brood upon her, and enrich
Earth with her shadow! I trust she will return.
These Romans dare not violate the Temple.
No, I must lure my game into the camp.
A woman I could live and die for. What!
Die for a woman, what new faith is this?
I am not mad, not sick, not old enough
To doat on one alone. Yes, mad for her,
Camma the stately, Camma the great-hearted,
So mad, I fear some strange and evil chance
Coming upon me, for by the Gods I seem
Strange to myself.

Re-enter **CAMMA**

CAMMA
Where is Antonius?

SYNORIX
Where? As I said before, you are still too early.

CAMMA
Too early to be here alone with thee;
For whether men malign thy name, or no,
It bears an evil savour among women.
Where is Antonius? [Loud.]

SYNORIX
Madam, as you know
The camp is half a league without the city;
If you will walk with me we needs must meet
Antonius coming, or at least shall find him
There in the camp.

CAMMA
No, not one step with thee.
Where is Antonius? [Louder.]

SYNORIX [advancing towards her]
Then for your own sake,
Lady, I say it with all gentleness,

And for the sake of Sinnatus your husband,
I must compel you.

CAMMA [drawing her dagger]
Stay!—too near is death.

SYNORIX [disarming her]
Is it not easy to disarm a woman?

Enter **SINNATUS** [seizes him from behind by the throat]

SYNORIX [throttled and scarce audible]
Rome! Rome!

SINNATUS
Adulterous dog!

SYNORIX [stabbing him with **CAMMA'S** dagger]
What! will you have it?

[**CAMMA** utters a cry and runs to **SINNATUS**

SINNATUS [falls backward]
I have it in my heart—to the Temple—fly—
For my sake—or they seize on thee. Remember!
Away—farewell!

[Dies.

CAMMA [runs up the steps into the Temple, looking back]
Farewell!

SYNORIX [seeing her escape]
The women of the Temple drag her in.
Publius! Publius! No,
Antonius would not suffer me to break
Into the sanctuary. She hath escaped.

[Looking down at **SINNATUS**

'Adulterous dog!' that red-faced rage at me!
Then with one quick short stab—eternal peace.
So end all passions. Then what use in passions?
To warm the cold bounds of our dying life
And, lest we freeze in mortal apathy,
Employ us, heat us, quicken us, help us, keep us
From seeing all too near that urn, those ashes
Which all must be. Well used, they serve us well.

I heard a saying in Egypt, that ambition
Is like the sea wave, which the more you drink,
The more you thirst—yea—drink too much, as men
Have done on rafts of wreck—it drives you mad.
I will be no such wreck, am no such gamester
As, having won the stake, would dare the chance
Of double, or losing all. The Roman Senate,
For I have always play'd into their hands,
Means me the crown. And Camma for my bride—
The people love her—if I win her love,
They too will cleave to me, as one with her.
There then I rest, Rome's tributary king.

[Looking down on **SINNATUS**

Why did I strike him?—having proof enough
Against the man, I surely should have left
That stroke to Rome. He saved my life too. Did he?
It seem'd so. I have play'd the sudden fool.
And that sets her against me—for the moment.
Camma—well, well, I never found the woman
I could not force or wheedle to my will.
She will be glad at last to wear my crown.
And I will make Galatia prosperous too,
And we will chirp among our vines, and smile
At bygone things till that [pointing to **SINNATUS**] eternal peace.
Rome! Rome!

Enter **PUBLIUS** and **SOLDIERS**.

Twice I cried Rome. Why came ye not before?

PUBLIUS
Why come we now? Whom shall we seize upon?

SYNORIX [pointing to the body of **SINNATUS**]
The body of that dead traitor Sinnatus.
Bear him away.

[Music and Singing in Temple.

ACT II

SCENE I

—Interior of the Temple of Artemis. Small gold gates on platform in front of the veil before the colossal statue of the Goddess, and in the centre of the Temple a tripod altar, on which is a lighted lamp. Lamps [lighted] suspended between each pillar. Tripods, vases, garlands of flowers, etc., about stage. Altar at back close to Goddess, with two cups. Solemn music. Priestesses decorating the Temple.

[The Chorus of **PRIESTESSES** sing as they enter.]

Artemis, Artemis, hear us, O Mother, hear us, and bless us!
Artemis, thou that art life to the wind, to the wave, to the glebe, to the fire!
Hear thy people who praise thee! O help us from all that oppress us!
Hear thy priestesses hymn thy glory! O yield them all their desire!

PRIESTESS
Phoebe, that man from Synorix, who has been
So oft to see the Priestess, waits once more
Before the Temple.

PHOEBE
We will let her know.
[Signs to one of the Priestesses, who goes out.
Since Camma fled from Synorix to our Temple,
And for her beauty, stateliness, and power,
Was chosen Priestess here, have you not mark'd
Her eyes were ever on the marble floor?
To-day they are fixt and bright—they look straight out.
Hath she made up her mind to marry him?

PRIESTESS
To marry him who stabb'd her Sinnatus.
You will not easily make me credit that.

PHOEBE
Ask her.

Enter **CAMMA** as Priestess [in front of the curtains]

PRIESTESS
You will not marry Synorix?

CAMMA
My girl, I am the bride of Death, and only
Marry the dead.

PRIESTESS
Not Synorix then?

CAMMA
My girl,

At times this oracle of great Artemis
Has no more power than other oracles
To speak directly.

PHOEBE
Will you speak to him,
The messenger from Synorix who waits
Before the Temple?

CAMMA
Why not? Let him enter.
[Comes forward on to step by tripod.

Enter a **MESSENGER.**

MESSENGER [kneels]
Greeting and health from Synorix! More than once
You have refused his hand. When last I saw you,
You all but yielded. He entreats you now
For your last answer. When he struck at Sinnatus—
As I have many a time declared to you—
He knew not at the moment who had fasten'd
About his throat—he begs you to forget it.
As scarce his act:—a random stroke: all else
Was love for you: he prays you to believe him.

CAMMA
I pray him to believe—that I believe him.

MESSENGER
Why that is well. You mean to marry him?

CAMMA
I mean to marry him—if that be well.

MESSENGER
This very day the Romans crown him king
For all his faithful services to Rome.
He wills you then this day to marry him,
And so be throned together in the sight
Of all the people, that the world may know
You twain are reconciled, and no more feuds
Disturb our peaceful vassalage to Rome.

CAMMA
To-day? Too sudden. I will brood upon it.
When do they crown him?

MESSENGER
Even now.

CAMMA
And where?

MESSENGER
Here by your temple.

CAMMA

Come once more to me
Before the crowning,—I will answer you.

[Exit **MESSENGER**.

PHOEBE
Great Artemis! O Camma, can it be well,
Or good, or wise, that you should clasp a hand
Red with the sacred blood of Sinnatus?

CAMMA
Good! mine own dagger driven by Synorix found
All good in the true heart of Sinnatus,
And quench'd it there for ever. Wise!
Life yields to death and wisdom bows to Fate,
Is wisest, doing so. Did not this man
Speak well? We cannot fight imperial Rome,
But he and I are both Galatian-born,
And tributary sovereigns, he and I
Might teach this Rome—from knowledge of our people—
Where to lay on her tribute—heavily here
And lightly there. Might I not live for that,
And drown all poor self-passion in the sense
Of public good?

PHOEBE
I am sure you will not marry him.

CAMMA
Are you so sure? I pray you wait and see.

[Shouts [from the distance], 'Synorix! Synorix!'

CAMMA
Synorix, Synorix! So they cried Sinnatus
Not so long since—they sicken me. The One
Who shifts his policy suffers something, must

Accuse himself, excuse himself; the Many
Will feel no shame to give themselves the lie.

PHOEBE
Most like it was the Roman soldier shouted.

CAMMA
Their shield-borne patriot of the morning star
Hang'd at mid-day, their traitor of the dawn
The clamour'd darling of their afternoon!
And that same head they would have play'd at ball with
And kick'd it featureless—they now would crown.

[Flourish of trumpets.

Enter a Galatian **NOBLEMAN** with crown on a cushion.

NOBLE [kneels]
Greeting and health from Synorix. He sends you
This diadem of the first Galatian Queen,
That you may feed your fancy on the glory of it,
And join your life this day with his, and wear it
Beside him on his throne. He waits your answer.

CAMMA
Tell him there is one shadow among the shadows,
One ghost of all the ghosts—as yet so new,
So strange among them—such an alien there,
So much of husband in it still—that if
The shout of Synorix and Camma sitting
Upon one throne, should reach it, it would rise
He!... HE, with that red star between the ribs,
And my knife there—and blast the king and me,
And blanch the crowd with horror. I dare not, sir!
Throne him—and then the marriage—ay and tell him
That I accept the diadem of Galatia—

[All are amazed.

Yea, that ye saw me crown myself withal.

[Puts on the crown.

I wait him his crown'd queen.

NOBLE
So will I tell him.

[Exit.

Music. Two **PRIESTESSES** go up the steps before the shrine, draw the curtains on either side [discovering the Goddess], then open the gates and remain on steps, one on either side, and kneel. A PRIESTESS goes off and returns with a veil of marriage, then assists **PHOEBE** to veil **CAMMA**. At the same time **PRIESTESSES** enter and stand on either side of the Temple. **CAMMA** and all the **PRIESTESSES** kneel, raise their hands to the Goddess, and bow down.

[Shouts, 'Synorix! Synorix!' All rise.

CAMMA
Fling wide the doors, and let the new-made children
Of our imperial mother see the show.

[Sunlight pours through the doors.

I have no heart to do it. [To **PHOEBE**] Look for me!

[Crouches. **PHOEBE** looks out.

[Shouts, 'Synorix! Synorix!'

PHOEBE
He climbs the throne. Hot blood, ambition, pride
So bloat and redden his face—O would it were
His third last apoplexy! O bestial!
O how unlike our goodly Sinnatus.

CAMMA [on the ground]
You wrong him surely; far as the face goes
A goodlier-looking man than Sinnatus.

PHOEBE [aside]
How dare she say it? I could hate her for it
But that she is distracted.

[A flourish of trumpets.

CAMMA
Is he crown'd?

PHOEBE
Ay, there they crown him.

[Crowd without shout, 'Synorix! Synorix!'

[A **PRIESTESS** brings a box of spices to **CAMMA**, who throws them on the altar-flame.

CAMMA

Rouse the dead altar-flame, fling in the spices,
Nard, Cinnamon, amomum, benzoin.
Let all the air reel into a mist of odour,
As in the midmost heart of Paradise.
Lay down the Lydian carpets for the king.
The king should pace on purple to his bride,
And music there to greet my lord the king.

[Music.

[To **PHOEBE**] Dost thou remember when I wedded Sinnatus?
Ay, thou wast there—whether from maiden fears
Or reverential love for him I loved,
Or some strange second-sight, the marriage cup
Wherefrom we make libation to the Goddess
So shook within my hand, that the red wine
Ran down the marble and lookt like blood, like blood.

PHOEBE

I do remember your first-marriage fears.

CAMMA

I have no fears at this my second marriage.
See here—I stretch my hand out—hold it there.
How steady it is!

PHOEBE

Steady enough to stab him!

CAMMA

O hush! O peace! This violence ill becomes
The silence of our Temple. Gentleness,
Low words best chime with this solemnity.

Enter a procession of **PRIESTESSES** and **CHILDREN** bearing garlands and golden goblets, and strewing flowers.

Enter **SYNORIX** [as King, with gold laurel-wreath crown and purple robes], followed by **ANTONIUS, PUBLIUS,** Noblemen, Guards, and the Populace.

CAMMA

Hail, King!

SYNORIX

Hail, Queen!
The wheel of Fate has roll'd me to the top.
I would that happiness were gold, that I

Might cast my largess of it to the crowd!
I would that every man made feast to-day
Beneath the shadow of our pines and planes!
For all my truer life begins to-day.
The past is like a travell'd land now sunk
Below the horizon—like a barren shore
That grew salt weeds, but now all drown'd in love
And glittering at full tide—the bounteous bays
And havens filling with a blissful sea.
Nor speak I now too mightily, being King
And happy! happiest, Lady, in my power
To make you happy.

CAMMA
Yes, sir.

SYNORIX
Our Antonius,
Our faithful friend of Rome, tho' Rome may set
A free foot where she will, yet of his courtesy
Entreats he may be present at our marriage.

CAMMA
Let him come—a legion with him, if he will.
[To **ANTONIUS**] Welcome, my lord Antonius, to our Temple.
[To **SYNORIX**] You on this side the altar.
[To **ANTONIUS**] You on that.
Call first upon the Goddess, Synorix.

[All face the Goddess. **PRIESTESSES, CHILDREN**, Populace, and Guards kneel—the others remain standing.

SYNORIX
O Thou, that dost inspire the germ with life,
The child, a thread within the house of birth,
And give him limbs, then air, and send him forth
The glory of his father—Thou whose breath
Is balmy wind to robe our hills with grass,
And kindle all our vales with myrtle-blossom,
And roll the golden oceans of our grain,
And sway the long grape-bunches of our vines,
And fill all hearts with fatness and the lust
Of plenty—make me happy in my marriage!

CHORUS [chanting]
Artemis, Artemis, hear him, Ionian Artemis!

CAMMA

O Thou that slayest the babe within the womb
Or in the being born, or after slayest him
As boy or man, great Goddess, whose storm-voice
Unsockets the strong oak, and rears his root
Beyond his head, and strows our fruits, and lays
Our golden grain, and runs to sea and makes it
Foam over all the fleeted wealth of kings
And peoples, hear.
Whose arrow is the plague—whose quick flash splits
The mid-sea mast, and rifts the tower to the rock,
And hurls the victor's column down with him
That crowns it, hear.
Who causest the safe earth to shudder and gape,
And gulf and flatten in her closing chasm
Domed cities, hear.
Whose lava-torrents blast and blacken a province
To a cinder, hear.
Whose winter-cataracts find a realm and leave it
A waste of rock and ruin, hear. I call thee
To make my marriage prosper to my wish!

CHORUS
Artemis, Artemis, hear her, Ephesian Artemis!

CAMMA
Artemis, Artemis, hear me, Galatian Artemis!
I call on our own Goddess in our own Temple.

CHORUS
Artemis, Artemis, hear her, Galatian Artemis!

[Thunder. All rise.

SYNORIX [aside]
Thunder! Ay, ay, the storm was drawing hither
Across the hills when I was being crown'd.
I wonder if I look as pale as she?

CAMMA
Art thou—still bent—on marrying?

SYNORIX
Surely—yet
These are strange words to speak to Artemis.

CAMMA
Words are not always what they seem, my King.
I will be faithful to thee till thou die.

SYNORIX
I thank thee, Camma,—I thank thee.

CAMMA [turning to **ANTONIUS**]
Antonius,
Much graced are we that our Queen Rome in you
Deigns to look in upon our barbarisms.

[Turns, goes up steps to altar before the Goddess. Takes a cup from off the altar. Holds it towards
ANTONIUS. ANTONIUS goes up to the foot of the steps, opposite to **SYNORIX**

You see this cup, my lord.   [Gives it to him.

ANTONIUS
Most curious!
The many-breasted mother Artemis
Emboss'd upon it.

CAMMA
It is old, I know not
How many hundred years. Give it me again.
It is the cup belonging our own Temple.

[Puts it back on altar, and takes up the cup of Act I. Showing it to **ANTONIUS.**

Here is another sacred to the Goddess,
The gift of Synorix; and the Goddess, being
For this most grateful, wills, thro' me her Priestess,
In honour of his gift and of our marriage,
That Synorix should drink from his own cup.

SYNORIX
I thank thee, Camma,—I thank thee.

CAMMA
For—my lord—
It is our ancient custom in Galatia
That ere two souls be knit for life and death,
They two should drink together from one cup,
In symbol of their married unity,
Making libation to the Goddess. Bring me
The costly wines we use in marriages.

[They bring in a large jar of wine. **CAMMA** pours wine into cup.

[To **SYNORIX**] See here, I fill it.
[To **ANTONIUS**] Will you drink, my lord?

ANTONIUS
I? Why should I? I am not to be married.

CAMMA
But that might bring a Roman blessing on us.

ANTONIUS [refusing cup]
Thy pardon, Priestess!

CAMMA
Thou art in the right.
This blessing is for Synorix and for me.
See first I make libation to the Goddess,

[Makes libation.

And now I drink.

[Drinks and fills the cup again.

Thy turn, Galatian King.
Drink and drink deep—our marriage will be fruitful.
Drink and drink deep, and thou wilt make me happy.

[**SYNORIX** goes up to her. She hands him the cup. He drinks.

SYNORIX
There, Gamma! I have almost drain'd the cup—
A few drops left.

CAMMA
Libation to the Goddess.

[He throws the remaining drops on the altar and gives **CAMMA** the cup.

CAMMA [placing the cup on the altar]
Why then the Goddess hears.

[Comes down and forward to tripod. **ANTONIUS** follows.

Antonius,
Where wast thou on that morning when I came
To plead to thee for Sinnatus's life,
Beside this temple half a year ago?

ANTONIUS
I never heard of this request of thine.

SYNORIX [coming forward hastily to foot of tripod steps]
I sought him and I could not find him. Pray you,
Go on with the marriage rites.

CAMMA
Antonius—
'Camma!' who spake?

ANTONIUS
Not I.

PHOEBE
Nor any here.

CAMMA
I am all but sure that some one spake. Antonius,
If you had found him plotting against Rome,
Would you have tortured Sinnatus to death?

ANTONIUS
No thought was mine of torture or of death,
But had I found him plotting, I had counsell'd him
To rest from vain resistance. Rome is fated
To rule the world. Then, if he had not listen'd,
I might have sent him prisoner to Rome.

SYNORIX
Why do you palter with the ceremony?
Go on with the marriage rites.

CAMMA
They are finish'd.

SYNORIX
How!

CAMMA
Thou hast drunk deep enough to make me happy.
Dost thou not feel the love I bear to thee
Glow thro' thy veins?

SYNORIX
The love I bear to thee
Glows thro' my veins since first I look'd on thee.
But wherefore slur the perfect ceremony?
The sovereign of Galatia weds his Queen.
Let all be done to the fullest in the sight

Of all the Gods.
Nay, rather than so clip
The flowery robe of Hymen, we would add
Some golden fringe of gorgeousness beyond
Old use, to make the day memorial, when
Synorix, first King, Camma, first Queen o' the Realm,
Drew here the richest lot from Fate, to live
And die together.
This pain—what is it?—again?
I had a touch of this last year—in—Rome.
Yes, yes. [To **ANTONIUS**] Your arm—a moment—It will pass.
I reel beneath the weight of utter joy—
This all too happy day, crown—queen at once.
[Staggers.
O all ye Gods—Jupiter!—Jupiter!

[Falls backward.

CAMMA
Dost thou cry out upon the Gods of Rome?
Thou art Galatian-born. Our Artemis
Has vanquish'd their Diana.

SYNORIX [on the ground]
I am poison'd.
She—close the Temple door. Let her not fly.

CAMMA [leaning on tripod]
Have I not drunk of the same cup with thee?

SYNORIX
Ay, by the Gods of Rome and all the world,
She too—she too—the bride! the Queen! and I—
Monstrous! I that loved her.

CAMMA
I loved him.

SYNORIX
O murderous mad-woman! I pray you lift me
And make me walk awhile. I have heard these poisons
May be walk'd down.

[**ANTONIUS** and **PUBLIUS** raise him up.

My feet are tons of lead,
They will break in the earth—I am sinking—hold me—
Let me alone.

[They leave him; he sinks down on ground.

Too late—thought myself wise—
A woman's dupe. Antonius, tell the Senate
I have been most true to Rome—would have been true
To her—if—if—

[Falls as if dead.

CAMMA [coming and leaning over him]
So falls the throne of an hour.

SYNORIX [half rising]
Throne? is it thou? the Fates are throned, not we—
Not guilty of ourselves—thy doom and mine—
Thou—coming my way too—Camma—good-night.

[Dies.

CAMMA [upheld by weeping Priestesses]
Thy way? poor worm, crawl down thine own black hole
To the lowest Hell. Antonius, is he there?
I meant thee to have follow'd—better thus.
Nay, if my people must be thralls of Rome,
He is gentle, tho' a Roman.

[Sinks back into the arms of the **PRIESTESSES**.

ANTONIUS
Thou art one
With thine own people, and tho' a Roman I
Forgive thee, Camma.

CAMMA [raising herself]
'CAMMA!'—why there again
I am most sure that some one call'd. O women,
Ye will have Roman masters. I am glad
I shall not see it. Did not some old Greek
Say death was the chief good? He had my fate for it,
Poison'd. [Sinks back again.] Have I the crown on? I will go
To meet him, crown'd! crown'd victor of my will—
On my last voyage—but the wind has fail'd—
Growing dark too—but light enough to row.
Row to the blessed Isles! the blessed Isles!—
Sinnatus!
Why comes he not to meet me? It is the crown
Offends him—and my hands are too sleepy

To lift it off.

[**PHOEBE** takes the crown off.

Who touch'd me then? I thank you.

[Rises, with outspread arms.

There—league on league of ever-shining shore
Beneath an ever-rising sun—I see him—
'Camma, Camma!' Sinnatus, Sinnatus!

[Dies.

Alfred Lord Tennyson – A Short Biography

Alfred Tennyson was born on August 6th, 1809, in Somersby, Lincolnshire, the fourth of twelve children.

Much of his childhood was unhappy primarily caused by the mental instability of his father and the treatment he meted out to his wife and children. This was especially difficult as his father was also their tutor in classical and modern languages. Tennyson however did spend four years at a nearby school, Louth Grammar School [1816–1820] and then attended Scaitcliffe School, Englefield Green and King Edward VI Grammar School, Louth.

The young Tennyson showed and early and burgeoning talent for writing. At the age of twelve he had written a 6,000-line epic poem.

In the 1820s, however, Tennyson's father began to suffer frequent mental breakdowns that were exacerbated by alcoholism. One of Tennyson's brothers frequently had violent quarrels with his father, a second would be confined to an insane asylum, and another was later an opium addict.

Tennyson left home in 1827 to join his elder brothers at Trinity College, Cambridge. Rather than a longing for academic rigor it was more due to a desire to escape from Somersby. At Trinity he was with other young men also away from home and who knew little of the problems that had clouded his life for so long. Although he was very shy he was delighted to make new friends; he was handsome, intelligent, humorous, and a gifted impersonator.

Also in 1827, he and his brother Charles published Poems by Two Brothers. Although the poems were of teenage quality they attracted the attention of the "Apostles," a select undergraduate literary club led by Arthur Hallam. The "Apostles" provided Tennyson with both friendship and confidence as a poet although, after establishing a firm friendship with Hallam, he involved himself less and less with the group as a whole.

At the urging of both friends and his father the normally lazy Tennyson was prevailed upon to re-write an old poem and submit it in the competition for the chancellor's gold medal for poetry on the subject of Timbuctoo. Tennyson's "Timbuctoo" shows a deep passion for Romantic poetry. It won the chancellor's prize in the summer of 1829.

Now the best of friends Hallam and Tennyson, in the summer of 1830, were involved in a ridiculous jaunt to take money and secret messages to revolutionaries plotting the overthrow of the Spanish king. Tennyson's political enthusiasm was really only marginal compared to Hallam's, but he was glad to make his first trip abroad. Travelling through France to the Pyrenees, they met the revolutionaries at the Spanish border. Whilst politically their visions were dashed for Tennyson it opened his eyes and imagination to now exceed what he had already shown with his poem "Mariana."

The landscape and atmosphere of the Pyrenees generated such wonderful poems as "Oenone," which he began writing there; "The Lotos-Eaters;" inspired by a waterfall in the mountains; and "The Eagle;" invoked from the sight of the great hunters circling above them. Perhaps, above all, the small village of Cauteretz and the surrounding valley were more emotionally charged for Tennyson than any other place he visited. He would return many times over the next sixty years.

In 1830, Tennyson published Poems, Chiefly Lyrical and in 1832 he followed this with a volume entitled Poems. Reviews were, in the main, harsh and Tennyson was stung to such an extent that although he continued to write, and lay the foundations for many classics, he would not publish another book for nine years.

In 1833 occurred perhaps the pivotal moment in Tennyson's life and with it the birth of perhaps its greatest poetical remembrance.

That autumn, in what was meant as a gesture of gratitude and reconciliation to his father, Arthur Hallam accompanied him to the Continent. In Vienna Arthur died suddenly of apoplexy as a result of a congenital malformation of the brain.

Hallam's death, together with that of his father and a myriad of anxieties, stemming mainly from the belief that his family were grimly attached to poverty, and his ill-concealed fears that he might become a victim of epilepsy, madness, alcohol, and drugs, as others in his family had, or even that he might die like Hallam, conspired to upset the delicate balance of Tennyson's emotions. "I suffered what seemed to me to shatter all my life so that I desired to die rather than to live," he said of that period.

In 1836, at the age of twenty-seven, Tennyson became involved with Emily Sellwood, who was four years younger than he. It blossomed so that, by the following year, they considered themselves engaged.

From what remains of their correspondence it is clear that she was very much in love with him, although he apparently held back a little in spite of his affection for her. He seems not only to excessively worry about not having the financial means to marry, but also that he was falling into trances, which he thought were connected with the epilepsy from which other members of the family suffered. To marry, he thought, would mean passing on the disease to any children he might father.

In the summer of 1840 Tennyson broke off all relations with Emily. She continued to think of herself as engaged to him, but he abandoned any hope of marriage. To spare her further embarrassment, the story was put out that her father had forbidden their marriage because of Tennyson's poverty. His fears had forced him to abandon her.

During these years he used the dark feelings and events to write many of his finest works; "Ulysses," "Morte d'Arthur," "Tithonus," "Tiresias," "Break, break, break," and "Oh! that 'twere possible".

Perhaps eclipsing these was a group of individual poems taking shape that encapsulate his own feelings of loneliness as a result of Hallam's death. He continued to write and add to them for the next seventeen years before collecting them to form what some credit as the greatest of Victorian poems, In Memoriam [1850].

These years were also years of a nomadic, unsettled, transient lifestyle. He stayed with his mother and his unmarried brothers and sisters at the Somersby rectory until 1837, then moved to Essex and onwards to Kent; but often as not he could be found in London, staying in cheap hotels or with friends who lived there. He was lonely, despondent, drank and smoked to excess. Many friends thought that his poetic vision had failed, that his life would be just unrealised potential.

But Tennyson amidst his shambolic life was still writing, still producing works that would create an unmatched legacy amongst Victorian poets.

In 1842 Tennyson published again for the first time in many years with Poems [in two volumes], a complete critical and popular success.

Against this success Tennyson's business ventures were nothing that would inspire any confidence. Repeatedly worried about revenues and finances he invested almost £4,000 of his patrimony in a venture to manufacture cheap wood carvings by steam driven machines. In 1842 the business had failed and with it Tennyson's investment. It so debilitated his moods that the next year, 1843, he had to go into a "hydropathic" establishment for seven months of treatment in the hope of curing his depression.

Over the next five years he would try this treatment several times. The treatment itself seems, to us today at least, to be draconian; constant wrappings in cold, wet sheets, and abstinence from tobacco and alcohol. For a while this seemed to help and the effects would continue for a short time before the renewed appeal of drinking and smoking would start the cycle over.

A far better treatment for his ills was the £2,000 he received from an insurance policy upon the death of the organiser of the woodcarving scheme.

In 1845 Tennyson was granted a government civil list pension of £200 a year in recognition of both his poetic achievements and his financial need. Whilst his engrained habits of worry over finances was effectively relieved he continued to worry about what he thought was personal poverty and this fear would continue even when his poetry had made him wealthy.

Life for Tennyson was becoming increasingly more productive and more lucrative. By 1849 The Princess had been published and he was now offered a large advance from his publisher on the proviso that he assemble his elegies on Hallam into one complete poem.

Tennyson had now also resumed his relationship with Emily Sellwood and by the following year was talking again of marrying her.

In the Spring of 1850 The Poet Laureate William Wordsworth died and a new Laureate was needed for the Nation. Life was about to get very good indeed for Tennyson.

On June 1st 1850 In Memoriam was published, and later that month he and Emily were married at Shiplake Church. After a protracted four-month honeymoon in the Lake District, Tennyson returned south to find that the publication of In Memoriam had made him, without question, the major living poet.

Emily was now thirty-seven years old and of delicate health, but she had great determination; she quickly assumed control of the running of all the practical parts of her husband's life leaving him free to concentrate on his writing.

Tennyson may have fretted at the loss of his less structured life style and with it the responsibilities of marriage and parenting but they were both happy with their lives. Three sons were born, of whom two, Hallam and Lionel, survived.

The publication of In Memoriam ensured that Tennyson became one of Britain's most popular poets. And now further success would be heaped upon him.

It seemed certain that Tennyson would be nominated as Wordsworth's successor as Laureate. Tennyson knew that the prince consort, who advised the queen on such matters, was an admirer of his, and the night before receiving the letter offering the post, he dreamed that the prince kissed him on the cheek, and that he responded, "Very kind but very German."

At the age of 41, Tennyson had established himself as the most popular and esteemed poet of the Victorian era. The money from his poetry [often now exceeding 10,000 pounds per year] allowed him to purchase a house in the country and to write in relative seclusion. His appearance—a large and bearded man, he regularly wore a cloak and a broad brimmed hat—enhanced his notoriety.

In 1859, Tennyson published the first poems of Idylls of the Kings, reviews were not all complimentary but sales were. 40,000 copies were printed and within a fortnight a quarter of these were sold; it was a pattern that repeated itself with every following volume.

In 1884, he accepted a peerage, becoming Alfred Lord Tennyson, the name by whom all now know him.

The rest of his life was spent in the glow of love that the public give to a distinguished man who has reached a great age. He continued to write poetry almost as frequently as in his younger days, and though some of it lacked the spontaneity of earlier years, there were often masterpieces that mocked the passing years. Many of the finest poems of his old age were written in memory of his friends as they passed, leaving him increasingly alone.

Of all the blows of mortality, the cruelest was the death from "jungle fever" of his younger son, Lionel, who had fallen ill in India and was returning by ship to England. Lionel died in the Red Sea, and his body was put into the waves—

"Beneath a hard Arabian moon
And alien stars."

It took Tennyson two years to recover sufficiently to write this poem; "To the Marquis of Dufferin and Ava," [1889] who had been Lionel's host in India. Hauntingly, the poem is written in the same meter as In Memoriam, that masterpiece of his youth celebrating the death of another beloved young man.

Lionel's death was the climax of Tennyson's sense of loss, and from that time until his own death he searched for the proofs of immortality, even experimenting with spiritualism. His poetry of this period is saturated with this search, sometimes in questioning, sometimes in dogmatic assertion that scarcely hides the fear underlying it. Yet there were moments of calm as reflected in "Demeter and Persephone," in which he uses the classical legend as a herald of the truth of Christianity. And there was, of course, "Crossing the Bar," written in only a few minutes as he sailed across the narrow waters separating the Isle of Wight from the mainland.

In the last two years of his life; when he was too weak to write his poetry down, his son or wife would copy it for him.

The year before his death he wrote a simple and delicate little poem, "June Heather and Bracken," as a devotion of love to Emily, his faithful wife; to her he dedicated his last volume of poetry, which was published a fortnight after his death.

On October 6th, 1892, an hour or so after midnight, surrounded by his family, he died at Aldworth. It is said that the moonlight was streaming through the window and Tennyson himself had his finger holding open a volume of Shakespeare.

He was buried in Westminster Abbey.

Alfred Lord Tennyson – A Concise Bibliography

Poems by Two Brothers, [1827]
Timbuctoo: A Poem [in Blank Verse] [1829]
Poems, Chiefly Lyrical [1830]
Poems [1832]
Poems, 2 volumes [1842]
The Princess: A Medley [1847]
In Memoriam, A.H.H. [1849]
Ode on the Death of the Duke of Wellington [1852]
Maud, and Other Poems [1855]
Idylls of the King [1859]
Enoch Arden, etc. [1862/1864]
The Holy Grail and Other Poems [1869]
Gareth and Lynette Etc. [1872]
Queen Mary: A Drama [1875]
Harold: A Drama [1876]
Montenegro [1877]
Ballads and Other Poems [1880]
Becket [1884]
The Cup and The Falcon [1884]

Tiresias and Other Poems [1885]
Locksley Hall Sixty Years After, Etc. [1886]
Demeter and Other Poems [1889]
The Foresters, Robin Hood and Maid Marian [1892]
The Death of Oenone, Akbar's Dream, and Other Poems [1892]

www.ingramcontent.com/pod-product-compliance
Lightning Source LLC
Chambersburg PA
CBHW060100050426
42448CB00011B/2560